SCHIRMER PERFORMANCE EDITIONS

KABALEVSKY
THIRTY PIECES FOR CHILDREN
Opus 27

Edited by Richard Walters
Recorded by Jeffrey Biegel

T0071596

To access companion recorded performances online, visit:
www.halleonard.com/mylibrary

Enter Code
1320-5072-7097-8875

On the cover:
Russian Scene (1904)
by Wassily Kandinsky (1866–1944)

ISBN 978-1-4234-5810-4

G. SCHIRMER, Inc.

DISTRIBUTED BY

HAL•LEONARD®
7777 W. BLUEMOUND RD. P.O. BOX 13819 MILWAUKEE, WI 53213

www.musicsalesclassical.com
www.halleonard.com

CONTENTS

The price of this publication includes access to companion recorded performances online, for download or streaming, using the unique code found on the title page. Visit www.halleonard.com/mylibrary and enter the access code.

HISTORICAL NOTES

DMITRI KABALEVSKY (1904–1987)

"Art shapes the man, his heart and mind, his feelings and convictions—the whole of his spiritual world. More than that art influences the development of society" —Dmitri Kabalevsky

Kabalevsky was born in St. Petersburg the son of a mathematician. Dmitri not only learned to play the piano, but also was a competent poet and painter as well. Facing financial difficulties, the family moved to Moscow following the October Revolution of 1917. Economic conditions in Russia were dire following World War I. In the ensuing political upheaval, work was hard to find. The Kabalevskys struggled as part of the working poor. Dmitri assisted in bringing in income, beginning to give piano lessons at 15 and playing for silent films at the theatre. He also held odd jobs, including delivering mail and drawing placards for shop windows.

In 1918, Kabalevsky began studying piano and art at the Scriabin Institute. His father wanted him to focus on economics and become a mathematician, but music quickly won the young boy's passions. He soon began teaching at the institute. Kabalevsky enrolled at the Moscow conservatory in 1925 studying composition and piano.

At the conservatory Kabalevsky joined two musical groups. The Proizvodstvennyi Kollektiv was a conservative, pro-Lenin organization. The Association of Contemporary Musicians was a progressive, avant-garde group. Hardly ten years after the Revolution and the uncertainty of political stability, Kabalevsky deliberately formed relationships with both political camps. This diplomacy would make him one of the most powerful musical voices in the USSR.

Kabalevsky graduated from the conservatory in 1930 and began lecturing there soon after. In 1932, when the Communist Party dissolved all music organizations and created the Union of Soviet Composers, Kabalevsky stepped up as a founding member, using his ties with the more conservative Proizvodstvennyi Kollektiv to demonstrate his commitment to traditional Russian values and the Russian people. He became a writer

for the magazine *Muzgiz* and for *Moscow Radio*. These platforms allowed him to endorse Russian music that was "for the people" and condemn the music that was overly "formalist," a catch-all phrase used by Communist leaders to identify art intended for the "intellectual connoisseurs or sophisticated esoterics," ideas the Communists lifted almost directly from Tolstoy's *What is Art?*

Kabalevsky married in 1931, divorced in 1935, and remarried in 1937. During this time, in addition to his continued teaching appointment at the Moscow conservatory, he became the senior editor of *Muzgiz*. In 1939, he gained full professorship at the conservatory. Throughout the 1930s, Kabalevsky began to take a more prominent role in the Union of Soviet Composers and in the 1940s, became editor of the *Sovetskaya Muzika* as well as the Chief of the Board of Feature Broadcasting on *Moscow Radio* after joining the Communist Party. The Soviet government considered him important enough to be evacuated during World War II to Sverdlovsk (now Yekaterinburg) as Hitler's army drew closer to Moscow.

Following World War II, the Conference of Musicians at the Central Committee of the All-Union Communist Party was held in 1948 to outline a policy known as Socialist Realism, the official name of Marxist art and aesthetic theory. The policy asked artists to create art that is "comprehensible to the masses, and inspires the people with admiration for the dignity of the working man and his task of building Communism."[1] The conference and ensuing policy spawned widespread questioning of anyone whose music was not politically correct. There were interrogations and threats to those who would not change their style to serve the party. Somehow Kabalevsky managed to get his name removed from the list of potentially "harmful" composers. He is the only prominent Russian composer of the time to avoid interrogation.

Kabalevsky published just over 100 pieces and wrote far more during his life. Most famous today are his suite *The Comedians*, his violin concerto, and several piano collections. The style is always conservative, approachable, and clear, yet quirky, inventive, and light-hearted. Kabalevsky's music demonstrates a master composer capable of disciplined and limited use of material based on a few fundamentals, like a painter that deliberately uses a limited palate of colors.

Beginning in the 1950s until his death, Kabalevsky wrote little music. Instead, he became heavily involved in national and international pedagogical organizations. From 1952 until his death he served on the board of the Union of Soviet Composers of the USSR; in 1953 he became a member of the Soviet Committee for the Defense of Peace; in 1954, USSR Ministry of Culture; in 1955, World Peace Council; in 1961, United Nations Educational, Scientific and Cultural Organization International Music Council, Council of Directors of the International Society for Music Education. Later, he became a member of the Committee for Lenin Prizes for Literature and Art, the Head of the Council on Aesthetic Education, a deputy to the USSR Supreme Council, Honorary President of the Academy of Pedagogical Sciences in the USSR, and Honorary President of the International Society of Music Education.

During much of this time, Kabalevsky also gave lectures on radio, television, and at various functions in many different countries on music appreciation, pedagogy, and aesthetics.

Perhaps Kabalevsky's most enduring contribution to Soviet music education was his work with the Laboratory of Musical Education in the 1970s. He succeeded in compiling specific lesson plans to be implemented in all Soviet classrooms. It became a complete syllabus (texts, recordings, and detailed outlines of each lesson) for all music education in the country. He then went into the primary schools of Moscow to implement this system. The program focused on political indoctrination, moral education, and character training at its base. Eventually Kabalevsky retired from the conservatory and dedicated his full attention to the education of children in primary schools. He stated in 1974, "when I decided it was time to sum up my work in this [music education] field, I discovered that it was not the summing up, but the beginning of a new stage. I realized that all I had done was merely preparation for going into general schools not merely as a composer or lecturer, but as an ordinary teacher of music."[2]

Up to the last moments of his life Kabalevsky was furthering music education and peaceful relations between all people of all cultures. He died of a heart attack at a conference to which he was to deliver a lecture on the disarmament of world powers of their nuclear weapons.

In Frank Callaway's eulogy given a few days later, he summed up the great influence of the composer: "Kabalevsky believed and demonstrated that music cultivates the artistic tastes and the creative imagination of children, as well as their love of life, of people, of nature, of motherland, and fosters their interest in, and friendships toward, peoples of all nations."[3]

PERFORMANCE NOTES

Introduction to Kabalevsky's Music

"We live in a difficult—interesting but difficult—epoch, but still life is wonderful. Great art can only come from love for life, love for man. Art must serve society, the people must understand it. The love of man must be there." –Dmitri Kabalevsky.[4]

In his book *Music and Education: A Composer Writes About Musical Education*, Kabalevsky several times cites the quotation by Maxim Gorki that books for children should be "the same as for adults, only better."[5] This quotation is the guiding principle behind all of Kabalevsky's music for children. He did not want to compose simplified or dumbed-down adult art, but good art for children. This flowed very naturally out of his educational theories, that of teaching musical literacy rather than musical grammar, instructing how to listen to music, define shapes and structures, not just how to read or how to identify elements of music.

Building an educational framework, Kabalevsky's book *A Story of Three Whales and Many Other Things* identifies three archetypes as basic musical forms from which all other larger forms are generated and most accessible to children: song, dance, and march. The archetypes (or whales) become the bridges upon which children may enter the world of music. Nearly all of Kabalevsky's music for children can be understood as fitting into one of these categories.

Kabalevsky believed that "no piece of music, however short and modest, should pass by a child without touching his mind and heart."[6] And it is easy to hear in his pedagogical works that he was focusing on developing a real musical culture in children rather than just getting them to practice or learn scales.

Kabalevsky composed 253 pieces during his lifetime, of which 125 are for children. There are twenty piano collections containing 153 pieces specifically for pedagogical purposes. It is no wonder he has remained such a popular choice among piano teachers.

It is worth saying that Kabalevsky considered music to be for people of all ages. His specific emphasis was on creating good music first, then helping students understand the music. Even though the title refers to children, this collection continues in the tradition established by composers like Schumann and Tchaikovsky in creating well-crafted, approachable pieces that focus on specific pedagogical techniques that piano students of any age will find valuable.

Thirty Pieces for Children, Op. 27

The opus 27 pieces were written from 1937–1938 and revised in 1985. Because USSR copyrights were not recognized by many other countries for much of the last century, unauthorized editions of the pieces appeared from the 1940s into the 1980s. The 1985 edition was intended to be the authoritative edition. Since the establishment of copyright through the world, most unauthorized editions have been suppressed.

The pieces have a relatively narrow range of difficulty. They were not intended to be in progressive order of difficulty. Below is an approximate rearrangement of the pieces with consideration to their difficulty. Also included is the specific "whale" (see above) that each piece attempts to demonstrate.[7]

Easiest

No. 1:   Waltz (dance)
No. 2:   A Little Song (song)
No. 4:   At Night on the River (song)
No. 12:   Toccatina (song/toccata)

Lower Intermediate

No. 5:   Playing Ball (dance)
No. 6:   A Sad Story (song)
No. 7:   An Old Dance (dance)
No. 9:   A Little Fable (song)
No. 25:   Novelette (dance)

Upper Intermediate

No. 3:   Etude in A minor (march)
No. 8:   Lullaby (song)
No. 10:   Clowning (dance/toccata)
No. 13:   A Little Prank (march)
No. 14:   Scherzo (dance)
No. 15:   March (march)
No. 16:   Lyric Piece (song)
No. 17:   Meadow Dance (dance)
No. 18:   Sonatina (march/song)
No. 21:   The Chase (march)
No. 26:   Etude in A Major (dance/march)

Most Difficult

No. 11:   Rondo (march)
No. 19:   War Dance (dance)
No. 20:   Fairy Tale (song)
No. 22:   A Tale (song)
No. 23:   Snow Storm (dance/march)
No. 24:   Etude in F Major (dance)
No. 27:   Dance (dance)
No. 28:   Caprice (song)
No. 29:   Song of the Cavalry (dance)
No. 30:   A Dramatic Event (march)

Fingering

The fingering is primarily by Kabalevsky, with some additional editorial suggestions. Consideration has been given to a medium-sized hand with a few alternate fingerings for smaller hands. Performing smooth musical lines is the goal of any fingering with economy of motion usually the best solution.

Pedaling

The pedaling (primarily by Kabalevsky; additional editorial suggestions in a few spots) throughout is designed to assist the drama of each piece. Following these indications will help with the interpretation of each piece. In general, this is music that, unless indicated, should be played *without* pedal. Needless pedaling will quickly destroy the clarity of the compositions.

Tempos

No specific metronome markings were provided by the composer. However, the moods are very deliberately marked. The "whale" that each piece should create is generally obvious and will be the best guide for tempos. The recording offers one choice of tempo among a wide range of options. Be sure to explore a tempo that allows you to express the musical clarity and excitement.

Articulation

Kabalevsky's articulation is extraordinarily specific and integrally part of the composition. By following it precisely, phrasing and other musical elements generally fall into place very naturally. This is part of the genius of why these works are such wonderful teaching pieces. To ignore the detailed articulation and phrasing is to misrepresent the careful construction.

Notes on the Individual Pieces

1. Waltz

The piece is relatively quiet, using only the treble register until the very end, which creates a music-box quality. The tempo should definitely be felt in one rather than three. It is in a ternary form: the first sixteen measures may be thought of as unit A (two statements of the idea); measures 17–24, the B section; and measures 25–32, the return of A with a short 4-measure coda at the end. Make something of the markings in measures 13 and 14 to signal a new tonal direction. Playing them too timidly could sound like a mistake. You might choose to cleanly pedal each measure to achieve a very smooth effect. Another approach could be to not pedal at all, but requires the pianist to be especially graceful. Note that in the right hand of each measure, the two-note phrases end on a quarter note, whereas the left hand ends on an eighth note followed by an eighth rest. A danger in performance would be to play the hands equally short, clipping the quarter note in the right hand, which would destroy the melody.

2. A Little Song

Think of *Andantino* as an indication of a quarter-note, not a half-note tempo. There is a temptation to take this piece too quickly, and a short work like this would be minimized in substance. Also, the sadness would be lost. For such a short piece, Kabalevsky gives several quite specific dynamic changes which should be used to their fullest effect. It is clear from his phrasing that primarily legato, smooth playing is in order. Generally the composer's phrasing follows hand position. For instance in measure 1, the right hand plays the first five notes in a five-finger position; after that, when the hand lifts and moves to a new position, a new phrase begins. The same is true in measures 5 and 6 of the left hand, and also in measure 5–8 in the right hand. The piece is divided into four 4-measure phrases that each make up a section. The first and third are related and the second and fourth are related. Kabalevsky is such a master of motivic development, the two basic ideas of the movement interweave almost seamlessly, making it difficult to define a specific form for the piece. The final cadence comes as a surprise when it arrives at the final E-minor chord not on a down beat but on beat three of the penultimate measure.

3. Etude in A minor

This piece is a scale study in both chromatic and diatonic motion. This is a good companion piece for a student working intently on scales. Because the left hand is very simple, the right hand can focus on the passage work. Any unevenness in scale technique will be readily apparent. The piece will be dull if you do not pay attention to the composer's dynamics, which provide much contrast. In places such as measures 1–3, notice the feeling of quick up and down swells. There is a silent movie chase quality to the music. Even though in minor, it feels light-heartedly menacing. This is a ABA form with a truncated recapitulation: the first seven measures are the first section; measures 8–11, the second; measures 12–15 begin the repeat of the first section but head off to a dramatic ending with heavily accented chords. The recorded tempo is ambitious and may not be the final tempo for a student. Strive for steady evenness and fluidity rather than speed. This piece should begin at a practice tempo that will be quite a bit slower than the final performance tempo.

4. At Night on the River

This floating, lyrical, melancholy piece should never go beyond *mp* and should not be taken too quickly. By paying careful attention to the dynamic changes and the hairpin swells, a proper sense of phrasing can be achieved. There is a definite ternary form: three 6-measure statements of the melody with a slightly different ending to each. The phrasing should be carefully attended to in both hands with a slight lift between each phrase in the right hand. The ending should feel as if the music is drifting away. The boat has sailed into the distance and is only faintly heard. On the recording, the pianist has added a natural sounding *ritardando* in the last four measures, which is an optional but logical choice.

5. Playing Ball

This is a playful, light piece. The music jumps from one octave to the other. There is play between major and minor tonalities, and juxtaposition of various key centers. This is the composer's musical imagery of tossing the ball back and forth. It is very important to notice the dynamic shifts. These are clearly marked graduated dynamics that become clues to the structure, and provide interest in the otherwise similar material. In this ABA form, measures 1–16 for the first section; measure 17–38, the second; and finally a return of the first section with a different ending. Be sure to

notice the reversed dynamics in the repeat of the A section. The piece is built on two-bar phrases that are echoed in a different register. Pedaling is very carefully marked to emphasize the cadential figures that round off each eight-measure phrase. It is important to note that the pedal is lifted on the third beat of these measures to appropriately articulate the staccato. The obvious teaching topic is the constant repeated notes. Traditionally, in proper piano technique, one would alternate fingers on the repeated notes to get an even bounce of sound. On the recording, the pianist plays these repeated notes staccato to capture the character of the music.

6. A Sad Story

Find a beautiful legato sound that captures the pure sadness of the music. Emphasize the song-like quality; it may help to think of a voice singing the melody. A few specific details such as the markings in measures 6, 8, 10, etc., possibly indicate Kabalevsky had a text in mind. The stress markings are about giving individual notes expression and attention, like stressed words of a poem. The piece is built in 8-measure phrases with an added cadential chord at the end. Though not a strict form in terms of repeated material, it is more of a theme and variation. The melody is slightly altered with each statement. Be careful not to play too loudly until the *f* in measure 25. This will give the climax power and drama. It is interesting to note that there are no pedal markings until the *f* phrase which indicates that the piece should be played with legato fingers.

7. An Old Dance

The character of the piece is a rustic minuet. Minuets are generally courtly in character and restrained. This minuet has a lightness about it that is more boisterous than courtly. Think of a two-measure sway in the implied dance. As is usual for a minuet, it is in a ternary form with a varied repeat of the A section. The B section is much heavier; be sure to bring out that change of character from the lighter A sections. A musical challenge is what to do with the slurred staccatos in the melody of the first measure and in similar places. The composer has given very specific phrasing and articulation. Notice how he uses a stress mark in the forth measure to have the phrase gracefully taper off; again in measure 18. Another difficulty is the staccato marking above the ornamented notes in measure 1 and similar places. How is it to be played? The recording artist provides a possible interpretation, but there are others. Notice the pedaling is very sparsely marked. There is not a *ritardando* marked for the last two chords, but this might be considered. Plan your fingering carefully for the parallel thirds in measures 16–17 and 20–21.

8. Lullaby

This lullaby has a gentle, song-like quality, but also some concern or worry is hidden in the character of the music. *Cantabile* is an important clue to realizing the singing tone for the melody. Even though it is a through-composed piece and there is no set material that repeats in a conventional sense identifying the form, it is interesting how the composer uses the strict discipline of developing short motives to create a unified composition. The eighth-note figure is constant throughout and almost always forms a seventh chord of some type. One should be aware that the accompaniment figure is marked **p** in the beginning, which differs from the melody, is marked **mp**. The dynamics switch in measure 15 with the indication *cantabile e poco marcato*. An interesting facet of the piece is in measure 31, where Kabalevsky has indicated a little *ritardando* before the quasi-return of the opening material. The recording artist also adds a slight *ritardando* in measure 14. There is no pedaling indicated. One should consider playing without pedal and relying on legato fingering. Notice that the four eighth notes in the left hand (at the beginning) are phrased together. Every time the four eighth notes start, a new phrase begins. One of the challenges is that the two hands are not phrasing together.

9. A Little Fable

Fables don't always follow predictable paths. And this fable certainly takes surprising, quirky turns. There is an ambiguity of key and even, at times, the rhythmic structure of the phrase. One of the interesting consistent features of the piece is playing of the melody in octaves throughout without accompaniment. Every note is marked staccato except two notes in measures 2 and 4, the longest note values. The form is free, though it is clear that certain motivic ideas are repeatedly used and developed. The music becomes unexpectedly chromatic around measure 12 just before the loudest and most assertive part, setting up the drama. There is a mystery about this fable. What is it? Where is it headed? And this mysterious quality is the most important thing. The technical challenge is playing in octaves, hands together, maintaining balance and clarity. The staccato notes must be even. The composer probably intends separation between the notes, but a bit longer in duration than a staccato marking might suggest. Don't slap the keys; give them some weight and allow them to sound. Though there are no phrase marks, the dynamic indications will help to make a musically convincing performance. The pedal should not be used at all. The last three notes might have a slight *ritardando*.

10. Clowning

There is play throughout between major and minor tonalities and extreme dynamic contrast, hinting at the clowning nature of the piece. This is the kind of fast music that is very pianistic; it should fall naturally under the hands. The movement has its own momentum because the same finger patterns repeat throughout. To get the correct articulation and evenness of the basic motive, one should begin with slow practice using a metronome, and then work to a performance tempo. Looking at the page, one of the clues to the form are the dotted half notes. It is through-composed, but unified by motive. Some material does repeat but not in a strictly formal way. Pedaling is carefully marked and should be followed explicitly. The *una corda* is indicated in two places. This change of color in the sound creates interest in otherwise similar music. Once practiced, this piece will sound more difficult than it really is.

11. Rondo

A rondo is a sectional piece with multiple recurrence of the theme. The rondo theme is measures 1–4 with a varied recurrence in measures 9–16, and a literal repeat in measure 25–32. A secondary theme is in measures 5–8, and presented again in a transposed key in measures 17–20. Measures 21–24 might be thought of as a third theme or a variation of the second. The last two measures serve as a coda. As is typical for a rondo, the tonal relationship between the sections is important. The piece moves from C minor, through A minor, back to C minor, a quick trip to E minor, and finally returns to C minor. Juxtaposition of material and tonal centers create playfulness. Note that the piece is built on constant change of material: the heavy **mf** or **f**, intense hands moving the same direction, contrasted with the softer section that is more lyrical, with thirds in the right hand. There are contrasts in range: the heavy rondo theme is lower, the lyrical second theme is higher. Another unique aspect of the piece is that the articulation in the hands is completely different between the sections. The first theme should be played non legato; the second theme requires a smoother touch. The final two measures are also legato. Even though the piece is brief, it is really a sophisticated take on a rondo form.

12. Toccatina

One of Kabalevsky's best-known and certainly one of his most-performed pieces, this Toccatina is a fun show piece. A toccata is a virtuoso composition that shows brilliance, often with imitative features. The Italian diminutive "toccatina" is a miniature version. It is by nature a free form. However, this particular toccata is almost in a rondo form. The first four measures function as a quasi-rondo theme, repeated in measures 13–16 and 35–38. Kabalevsky unifies the piece with the rhythmic idea of the sustained left-hand melody and short staccato triads in the right hand in an inversion of the harmony implied by the left hand, using one of two patterns. Even in this free form, the composer has a strict rhythmic and textural unity. Notice that most of the time the top note of the right hand chord mirrors an octave above the left hand melody. The technique required is independence of hands: the left hand playing smoothly and the right hand playing staccato throughout. There are three sections of the piece where the left hand is not marked with phrasing: measures 31–34, 39–42, and 45–49. In these spots the left hand should be deliberately played with less legato than the rest of the piece. Use the dynamics to create an overall arch in the structure of the piece. The composer indicates no pedaling; the piece is best performed without pedal. Maintain an evenness of touch in the staccato chords of the right hand, and also ensure that all three fingers go down together and evenly to create a crisp chord. This piece should be practiced at a slow tempo, and then worked up to an allegretto. There is a danger in performance of going too fast. Allegretto is a contained tempo. Do not dash through the piece.

13. A Little Prank

The title indicates playfulness which is clearly in the music, and there are unexpected twists. The composer does this with harmony. This is an ABA form. The large sections of the piece begin in measures 1, 16, and 35. For the A sections, the right hand plays a five-note descending scale and the left hand answers with a fifth. The B section reverses that pattern; up a fourth (inversion of a fifth) with an ascending scale in the left hand, a mirror of the texture. Beginning with the pickup to measure 21 is a new idea that interrupts the texture. It is related to the motive of the answering fifths/fourths. The coda in measure 50 is closely related to this secondary idea. A pause with an accent in measure 33 sets up the return of A. The return of A is played *p* without rises and falls in dynamics. There is a danger to begin this piece too quietly. The music should build to the middle where it is the most chromatic, and then back off and die away to the end. The technical challenge is an even scale that is quick and light. *Vivace leggiero* means lively, brisk, lightly (faster than allegro). As with all faster pieces, it should be practiced slowly and built up to a performance tempo. No pedal throughout.

14. Scherzo

Scherzo means joke in Italian. Musically it translates to be a light and quick piece, generally in some metrical division of three. *Allegro scherzando* literally translates as happy kidding. Because it is a minor key scherzo, there is a sly quality. It requires a light approach. The piece is somewhat in a rondo form. A sections appearing in measure 1, 13, and 29, always signaled by ritardandos in the preceding measure. B sections beginning in measures 9 and 21. A brief coda begins in measure 34. There is a general pattern of rise and fall over short sections. However, this rise and fall ends in measure 29 with *pp* to the end. The technical challenge is executing exactly what the composer asks: slurred notes, staccato notes, etc. Unevenness will be easily exposed. Independence of voices is important in places like measure 2. There should be no pedal except for the last two measures. Listen to what the recording artist does with the staccato and pedal in the penultimate measure to inform a possible solution.

15. March

The title is the clue to the tempo. It is a quick march, quicker than a walking tempo. The first 4 measures are an introduction. The theme begins in measure 5. The B section begins in measure 29, and a literal repeat of the A section begins in measure 37. The last six bars are an extension of the introduction. The piece is primarily staccato with accents occurring occasionally; only in the B section are there any slurred notes at all. Create distinct differences in the accented, slurred, and staccato notes. The articulations become the clues to phrasing the piece in an interesting and compelling way. Pedal is very sparse. Evenness of touch is paramount. Practice slowly first before attempting the performance tempo on the recording. Note that the introduction and the coda are quite loud as compared to when the theme is presented in measures 5 and 37. Measures 27 and 28 are the only other loud places.

16. Lyric Piece

The music has a song-like character. It is certainly a piece about melody. Distinguish clearly the accompaniment and make the melody sing. The phrases are longer in this piece than in any other in the collection. There is a melancholy quality to the music, echoing the long melodies of Chopin or Grieg. The form is free, united by an easily-identifiable rhythmic motive in the left hand, and the melodic fragment outlining a minor triad. The melody begins as the pickup to measure 3. The sections are clear and related by melody and motive, but the composer takes us down some different paths of key, especially in measure 17, going from C-sharp minor, to F minor, to F-sharp minor, then back to the tonic. There is a modal implication in the introduction, with the D-natural, also returning at the end. It is a quiet piece never rising above a *mf*. Pedaling is very carefully marked. It would ruin the music to over pedal, which is a temptation. Notice the slight separation in articulation in the repeated eighth notes on the recording beginning in measure 3. Note how carefully it should be articulated. When the left hand in measure 12 and 27 takes over the melody, it is marked *mf* and *dolce*. Note how in measure 17 the harmony goes someplace completely unexpected. Kabalevsky sets it up in a very interesting way with the pause on the C-sharp.

17. Meadow Dance

This is music purely about melody and accompaniment. There is not one accidental in the entire piece. It is a simple, white-note music that suits a simple nature scene perfectly. Imagine a lovely day in the meadow without any strong winds, without clouds, a day of peaceful, serene gentleness. There are three sections (ABA): measures 3–10, measures 11–18, and measures 19–22. The return of the A section is truncated and spun out into a coda. An unusual feature is the jumping of the triads in the left hand which the composer marks staccato while pedaling. This context for staccato is about lightness, not necessarily indicating short duration. Listen to the recording for a possible interpretation. Two completely different textures are called for in each hand. The right hand is legato throughout with few exceptions. It is a quiet piece. Though the middle section is slightly louder, it never rises above a *mf*. The lack of dynamic changes affirms the serenity of the meadow.

18. Sonatina

It is surprising that the composer titled this brief piece sonatina. A sonatina is a sonata on a smaller scale, usually more than one movement. The composer has an abbreviated sonata form in mind but, as is the case in sonatinas, the development section is omitted or very brief. The first theme begins in measure 1, the second theme in measure 13. Return of the first theme occurs in measure 25, and the second theme in measure 33. Note that in measure 9, the first theme is transposed. The similar spot in the recapitulation (measure 31) is where the theme moves back to the tonic key, as you would expect in a sonata. You can see throughout that the left hand is almost always an accompaniment until the last measures. The staccato chords should be performed crisply throughout. The right-hand, single-note melody should be played with careful attention to the phrasing and articulation. A big clue in the

composer's intentions occurs when the rhythm moves from the dotted eighth and sixteenth to the undotted eighth notes. This implies smoother playing. Unlike the other pieces in this collection, not every note has articulation from the composer. He does not indicate articulation on the repeated notes. Perhaps he means a slight separation? He also does not provide articulation for the eighth-note scale in measures 7–8. *Portando* might be the intention. (If he intended legato, it would be indicated.) There are some *subito p* and *subito mf* scattered throughout. Draw attention to these events as they create sudden excitement. Pedal *only* in measures 7 and 31. The left-hand chords must be even and crisp. Clarity and the independence of the hands are the technical challenge. Longer phrases in this piece should be played expressively. Measures 40–41 should sound like one falling figure from hand to hand. No note should jump out especially when making the switch between hands. Note the *ritardando* in measure 24. It will guide you in the structure of the piece.

19. War Dance

As the title suggests, this movement should be played aggressively and rhythmically. Pay particular attention to which notes receive which kind of accent, and more importantly, which do not receive any accent. Do not play notes with the stress (the first note, for example) staccato. Notice that when this motive recurs in measure 15, it is with a stronger accent. Dynamic contrast makes this piece exciting and effective. Every note of the piece is derived very organically out of the first two bars. The structure might be thought of in three parts (ABA), the return of the first section being truncated, with an extended coda. The A section (measures 1–8) is *f*, the B section (measures 9–14) is *p* with a crescendo back to *f* for the second A section (measures 15–18). Because of the range of the return of A, and the additional voice in the left hand, it is a stronger statement than the first, though they are both marked *f*. Emphasize the *subito p* in measure 19 and the sudden burst of volume in measure 24, which dies away to nothing. The war dance ends much less aggressively than the beginning. Perhaps it is a political statement as the piece was composed just as Hitler was threatening various European countries that would result in World War II. Keep the piece very steady. Like any quick piece, practice at a slower tempo before a performance tempo is achieved.

20. Fairy Tale

A fairy tale story might take unusual, unexpected twists, but there is always a happy ending. This music captures that. The repeated notes in measure 1 and in similar places are an important part of the texture. The composer does not state it, but it feels possible to a bit of a swell into the second measure of this figure. These measures are not legato. They have weight and tone. The piece is divided into three sections (ABA): A measures 1–8, B measures 9–24, A measures 25–32 with a coda measures 33–end. The B section could be divided up into two parts as well: measures 9–16 and measures 17–24. The piece is unified by a left-hand pattern that continues throughout, wandering into and out of various tonal centers. The four eighth notes (always three down then one up) outline a triad or a seventh chord. The tempo, *andantino cantabile* is a clear signal that this music is about the singing right-hand melody. Even though pedaling is used throughout, you should practice without pedal to achieve clarity of touch, tone, and evenness. The left-hand figure requires much attention, and should be practiced alone to create a smooth bed of sound without accents or stresses

21. The Chase

Most pieces with "chase" in the title have one hand following the other. This is not the case here. There is sinister weight with menace. This is not a light-hearted chase. The structure is built in eight-measure phrases, loosely outlining an ABABA Coda form (almost a rondo). The obvious first characteristic is that the entire musical content is presented with hands playing the same notes, separated by two octaves. In both of the B sections (measures 9–16 and 25–32), the first four measures are answered by the second four measures. It feels as though the composer is deliberately ambiguous about the key. It would seem to be in a G minor modal key. He implies harmony, but none is given in a forthright way. He moves away from the initial key in the B section through many keys. The music has a fleet texture and must be played with a nimble touch. To play too heavy in the spots marked *f* will give the performance the wrong character. A lack of evenness between hands will be very exposed. If the left hand is lazy, it will be very apparent to any listener. The articulation is exactly the same for both hands. No pedaling. It would be against the character and inappropriate. The music falls very easily under the hands once it has been learned. Use a slow tempo for practice, then build up to the performance tempo.

22. A Tale

One of the longest pieces in the set, this tale is one of mystery and ambiguity in an altered reality. The deliberate monotony of the left-hand pattern suggests melancholy with a twist as the unexpected turns begin chromatically wandering around. When the middle section begins, it is as if the music turns to a happier character. There is an exuberance, almost as if the imposed containment in the A section has lifted. The prison walls open up to more freedom in the B section, then the gradual decent back into the melancholy and familiarity of the A section.

There is something going on in this tale. The music seems to evolve and wander, as if it is mutating. An obvious ABA form emerges, the B section beginning in measure 25 and the return of A, abbreviated and altered in measure 39. The A section is a right-hand melody with accompaniment. In the left hand, the rhythm stays the same for 23 measures only changing the pitches. In the B section, the hands are in tenths, the left hand harmonizing the right. A climax is reached on the high notes at the fortissimo in measure 34, falling away in measures 35–38, then transitioning back to A. In the coda, there are eighth notes in both hands for the first time. Notice careful and repetitive use of the pedal in the A section. Do not pedal during the B section. In measure 21, the left hand resolves to D rather than C-sharp as expected. Give this lack of resolution emphasis.

23. Snow Storm

A quick scurry in a snowstorm with the wind whipping around, this is a fun piece to play. The first and third notes of each measure are the most important, the melody that will guide us through the snowstorm. The music is in a free form, motivically built on four-bar phrases. Measure 1–20 feel like a first section. In measure 21, the material starts like the beginning, but goes someplace different. Kabalevsky travels to many different keys, as if wandering in the snow. We get to a familiar place in measure 69, and it feels like a recapitulation a few measures later, but the music goes somewhere else to the end using the same motivic idea. Because of the way it is written and the intended tempo, you do not have any choice in phrasing. The short phrases are organically built into the music. One might call this keyboard choreography. The hands are given very strict movements, dancing over the keys in this prescribed way. Getting a distinct sound in the left hand is a technical challenge so that it does not sound muddled or harried. To make a musical performance, you must play all dynamics as written. Without these nuances, the piece is monotonous rather than buoyant and full of motion and life. Played at a labored dynamic level, the music will sound relentless and dull. It is a technically demanding piece because it asks the pianist to maintain an even figure that is constant throughout. Obviously the recorded performance is a tempo to which to aspire. One needs to practice at a very slow tempo and gradually increase the speed once the piece has been mastered. After you master it, it will be easier to play at a faster tempo than a slow one. The pedal should not be used anywhere.

24. Etude in F Major

This etude is a brilliant showpiece; this music features arpeggios and scales. A very simple melody is outlined and decorated. By using the first note and the last two notes of the measure in the first few bars, you can see the simple descending melody. The piece is in a sonata-rondo form: ABCA. A is measures 1–8, B is measures 9–14, C is measures 15–37, which serves as a development, and the repeat of A occurs in measure 38 with a two-measure coda at the end. The pedaling is indicated very specifically, just one beat in each measure, which heightens the brilliance if precisely executed. Too much pedal will blur the notes. The articulation is also very specific. Notice how it changes at the repeat of the A section. Practice arpeggios while working on this piece to get the hands accustomed to the motion. The extraordinary tempo of the recording artist may not be attainable by all who attempt this piece. One can imagine this at a slightly slower tempo. Practice will need to begin at a much slower tempo.

25. Novelette

Novelette is a title invented by Schumann for his opus 21 for pensive, solemn music that tells a melancholy story. Kabalevsky had a story in mind that we cannot discover, but the emotional contour comes through. The left hand is accompaniment, a low sound answered by a mid-range sound in the second half of each measure. The right hand plays the melody, almost always doubled in thirds. This is a free form that feels like a song. Kabalevsky might have had words in mind as a compositional tool. An irregular phrase structure is held together by motivic development as the sad story wanders through various keys. Pedal carefully. Generally, pedal on every downbeat. In the right hand, use legato fingers wherever possible. Beginning in measure 24, the bass line moves chromatically up by step to the climax of the piece in measure 38. The artist on the recording takes some *rubato*, which is an option. One might also think of the relentless bass accompaniment as a reason to keep it steady throughout.

26. Etude in A Major

This piece is reminiscent of the previous etude (No. 24) in that it presents an arpeggio in one hand with a stepwise moving figure in the other hand. The emphasis in this etude is on finger strengthening, not as much on arpeggios. Like the other etude, the form is very similar to a sonata. Section A is through measure 18, section B in the relative F-sharp minor measures 19–34, the development measures 35–79, then the return of A in measures 80–92 with some slight adaptations, followed by a coda. The music features vivid articulation and combinations of articulation, such as quick slurs with carefully marked pedaling, staccatos, and two-note slurs. In the descending scales beginning in measure 37, be sure to play the accented notes with separation, no pedal. The composer sets the return of the opening material with a change of texture. He extends the scale motive with the accents as if to say "here it comes." As in all these piano pieces, Kabalevsky takes simple elements and builds on them in a disciplined way. He does not go off into unrelated material. It ends softly, not with a bang. The piece lies under the hands quite well. The trickiest part is the section that begins in measure 99. Carefully finger this passage. If the suggested fingering does not work for your hand, find something else. Like all nimble pieces, this needs to be practiced at a slow tempo, then gradually increase tempo to a performing tempo. If you cannot reach the tempo of the performing artist, you might choose one a bit slower.

27. Dance

The title implies movement and gracefulness. It would be interesting for a player to conjure an imaginary dance, as if you are playing for a dancer. The piece is structured like a rondo: ABACA. The first eight measures recur in the pick up to measures 17 and 39. The B section might be thought of as measures 9–16. The C section at the *Vivace*. Use no pedal to properly execute the staccatos, which appear on every note except in measures 25 and 26. It requires a great deal of precision to execute these staccatos cleanly and gracefully. Staccatos need a buoyant touch and a sense of phrase or they become stiff and rigid. Short notes do not mean a lack of phrase. The parallel thirds in the left hand of measure 25 are technically the most challenging and will require much practice.

28. Caprice

Caprice is a short piano piece of humorous character, usually in a ternary form. This piece follows that model in a broad sense, though the form does not fit as cleanly. The first thirty-two measures might be thought of as A (or as A and B); measures 33–50, the B section (or C); and from measure 51 to the end, the return of A an octave higher. It is a quirky piece, chromatic and modal. The D-natural in measure 8 gives a modal flavor. Kabalevsky moves from the opening key of E major to the relative C-sharp minor, implied in measure 17. We are clearly in a new key when we get to the second section at measure 33. The sustained notes outline the harmony in a basic way. This is a study in independence of fingers. In both hands a note is held down while playing staccato in the other voice. The right and the left hand play in octaves throughout. Like all of these miniatures, it is about precision. Be sure to strike the sustained note hard enough to carry though under the staccato notes, but without accenting too strongly. Play the staccato notes softly. The music requires very careful fingering, especially for the left hand in measures 21–24. Even the *ff* passage in measure 51 requires a lightness of touch. Use no pedal in this piece. The music is both playful and serious. The composer's playfulness is with chromaticism as well as with the staccato texture.

29. Song of the Cavalry

There is an aggressive nature to the piece that sounds like a pursuit, relentless in its mood. The A section begins with a melody in the left hand, accompanied by short staccato chords in the right hand on the off-beat. The B section begins in measure 26. After a short interlude, the texture changes and the melody is in the right hand. Measures 36–43 are very tricky and will take an extra amount of practice. This is also the section that is the most varied in terms of texture and complexity. The composer has told us at the top of the piece *senza pedale*, so no pedal. The texture is either staccato, accented, or short slurs of three or four notes. Even though there is an aggressive quality, it should not be too heavy, as it can easily become stodgy. Use a light touch. One of the fun things about the piece is the sudden changes in dynamics in measures 3, 11, 13, and many other places. The music begins in B-flat minor, makes its way to F minor in the B section, then to the parallel major (F major) which becomes the dominant of B-flat minor for the return to A. There is a traditional tonal harmonic relationship between the sections. At the return of A, the dynamics are different. Because of the key of the piece, much of the music is played on the black keys. It should be practiced at a slow tempo and built to the *allegro molto*.

30. A Dramatic Event

As the title suggests, this piece needs to be played with a great deal of drama. It has a gravity about it that is unique in this collection. No other piece has this amount of weight. What one notices immediately is the imitative nature between hands. Though it is not a fugue, it has a fugue-like quality, with fairly strict imitation, such as the canon from measures 1–17. The texture begins to change in measure 19. Then back to a canon until measure 24, when the hands are in unison at the octave for a stretch. At measure 34, the texture changes with the introduction of the repeated chords. The canonic section returns in measure 48. The structure is in spirit ABA. Notice that the composer modu-

lates through several keys in the B section before arriving in measure 48 in D-flat Major. The quick notes after the double dots are the clue to the texture of the piece. These cannot be lazy and must be precise in rhythm. Even with the jerky texture, the composer says legato, which means that the dotted note should be sustained, not punched. Be careful in measure 34 not to be too loud; you still have to crescendo into measure 48, so sustain the *f* for a while and go further. Bring out the bottom notes and the top notes of the chords through measure 48 as they progress by half step to the climax of the piece. This is an elegant, logical, chromatic progression to the arrival point, a loud D-flat chord. The performer on the recording chose to use some *ritardando* at the end of the piece. One might also choose to keep the tempo steady to the end. Tone is extremely important, and a beautiful full finger tone is the key to success. No banging! Too light of a touch will diminish the music. It takes rigorous finger work to make the canon be heard clearly. Note the overall points of arrival: the crescendo into measure 19, the crescendo into measure 34, and the climax at measure 48. Plan the drama around these points.

– Richard Walters, editor,
and Joshua Parman, assistant editor

Notes

[1] David Lawrence Forrest, *The Educational Theory of Dmitri Kabalevsky in Relation to His Piano Music for Children* (Ph.D. diss., University of Melbourne. 1996), 87.

[2] ibid., 36.

[3] ibid., 40.

[4] in an interview with *The New York Times,* October 27, 1957 "Optimistic Russian: Kabalevsky, in Speaking of His Fourth Symphony, Reveals Attitude to Life" (quoted in Forrest, 103).

[5] Dmitri Kabalevsky, *Music and Education: A Composer Writes About Musical Education* (London: Jessica Kingsley Publishers, 1988), 120.

[6] Forrest, 143.

[7] Forrest, 233–34, 345, 414–15.

References

Daragan, Dina Grigor'yevna. "Kabalevsky, Dmitry Borisovich," *The New Grove Dictionary of Music and Musicians*. ed. S. Sadie and J. Tyrrell. London: Macmillan. 2001.

Forrest, David Lawrence. *The Educational Theory of Dmitri Kabalevsky in Relation to His Piano Music for Children*. (Ph.D. diss., University of Melbourne. 1996).

Kabalevsky, Dimitri. *30 Piano Pieces for Young Players, Op. 27, Book 1.* Hamburg: Musickverlag Hans Sikorski GmbH & Co., 2006.

Kabalevsky, Dimitri. *30 Piano Pieces for Young Players, Op. 27, Book 2.* Hamburg: Musickverlag Hans Sikorski GmbH & Co., 2006.

Kabalevsky, Dimitri. *30 Piano Pieces for Young Players, Op. 27, Book 3.* Hamburg: Musickverlag Hans Sikorski GmbH & Co., 2006.

Kabalevsky, Dimitri. ed. Joseph Prostakoff. *30 Pieces for Children, Op. 27.* New York: G. Schirmer, Inc., 1968.

Kabalevsky, Dimitri. ed. John York. *30 Pieces for Children, Op. 27.* London: Boosey & Hawkes, 2001.

Kabalevsky, Dimitri. *Music and Education: A Composer Writes About Musical Education.* London: Jessica Kingsley Publishers, 1988.

Kabalevsky, Dimitri. ed. Keith Snell. *Thirty Pieces for Children, Op. 27.* San Diego: Neil A. Kjos Music Company, 1996.

Krebs, Stanley Dale. *Soviet Composers and the Development of Soviet Music.* New York: W. W. Norton & Company, 1970.

Maes Francis. trans. Arnold J. and Erica Pomerans. *A History of Russian Music: From Kamarinskaya to Babi Yar.* Berkley: University of California Press, 2002.

Thirty Pieces for Children
1. Waltz

Dmitri Kabalevsky
Op. 27

2. A Little Song

Dmitri Kabalevsky
Op. 27

3. Etude in A minor

Dmitri Kabalevsky
Op. 27

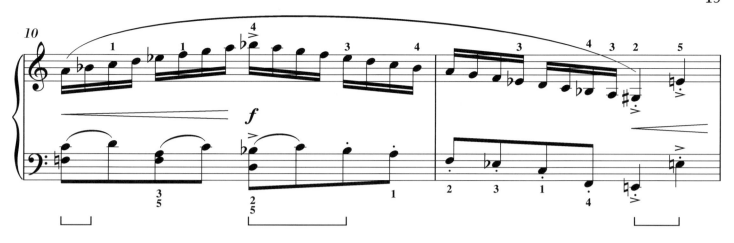

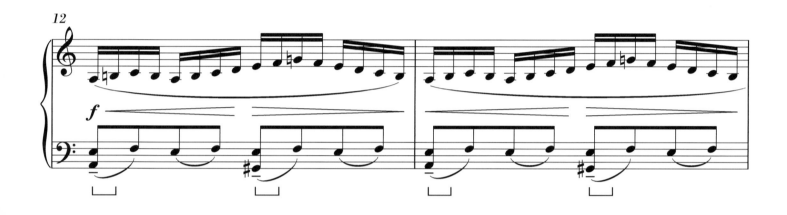

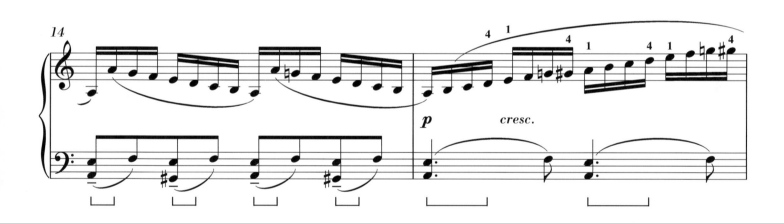

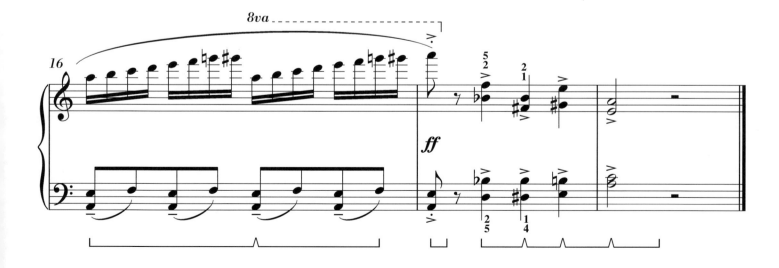

4. At Night on the River

Dmitri Kabalevsky
Op. 27

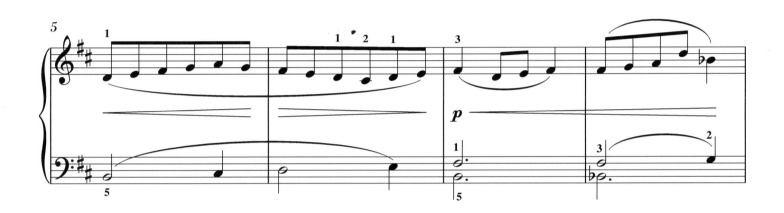

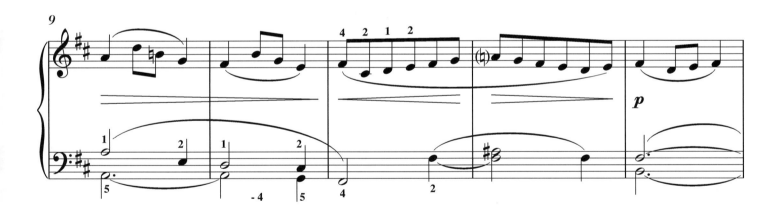

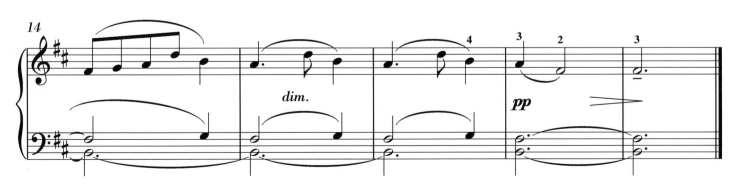

5. Playing Ball

Dmitri Kabalevsky
Op. 27

6. A Sad Story

Dmitri Kabalevsky
Op. 27

7. An Old Dance

Dmitri Kabalevsky
Op. 27

Tempo di Menuetto

8. Lullaby

Dmitri Kabalevsky
Op. 27

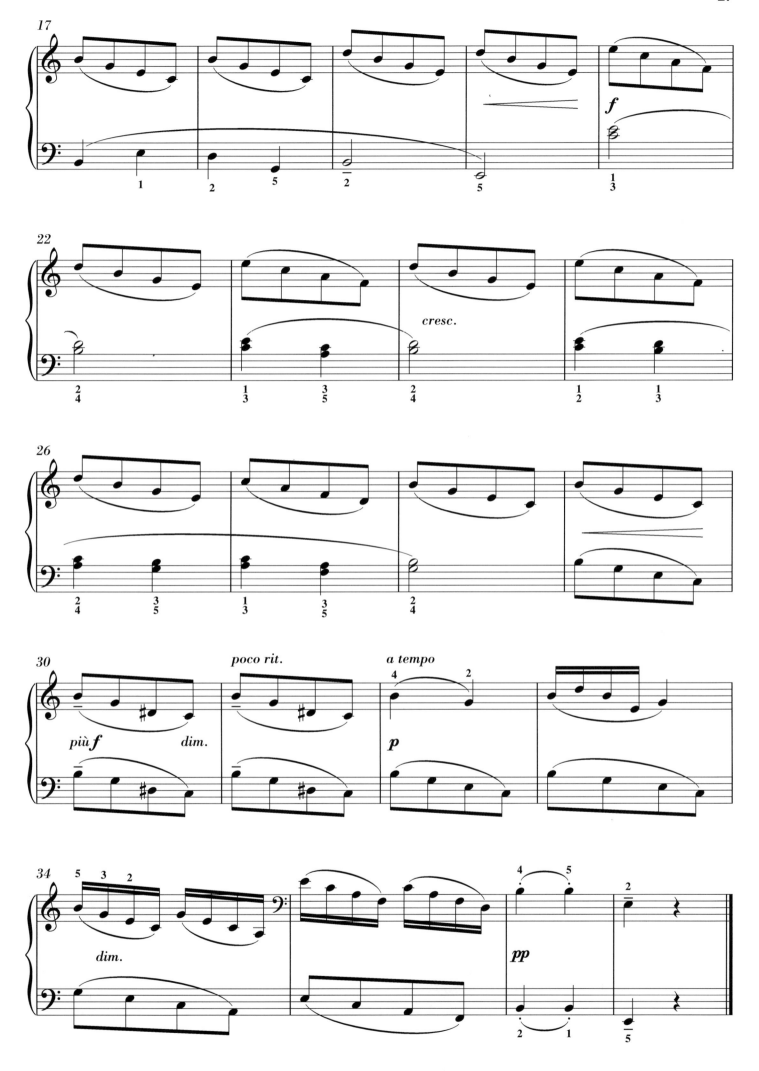

9. A Little Fable

Dmitri Kabalevsky
Op. 27

Allegro moderato

10. Clowning

Dmitri Kabalevsky
Op. 27

11. Rondo

Dmitri Kabalevsky
Op. 27

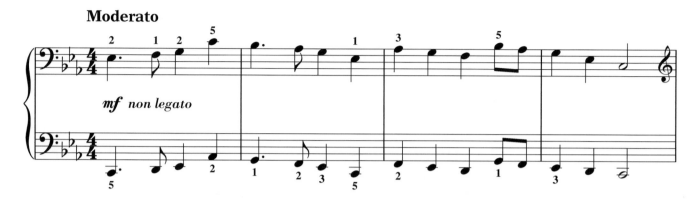

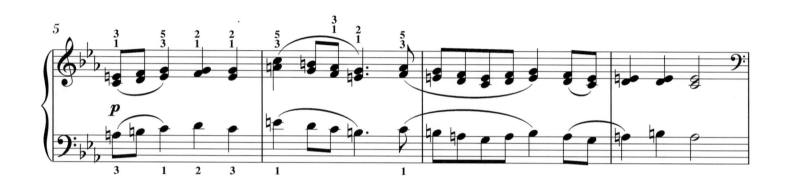

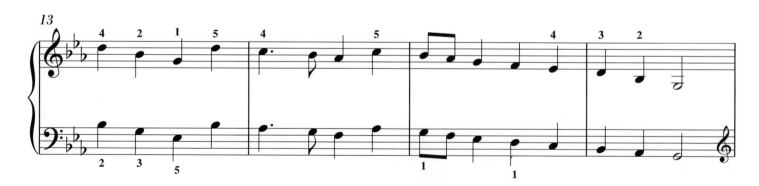

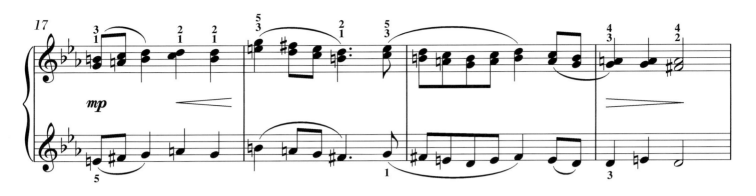

12. Toccatina

Dmitri Kabalevsky
Op. 27

13. A Little Prank

Dmitri Kabalevsky
Op. 27

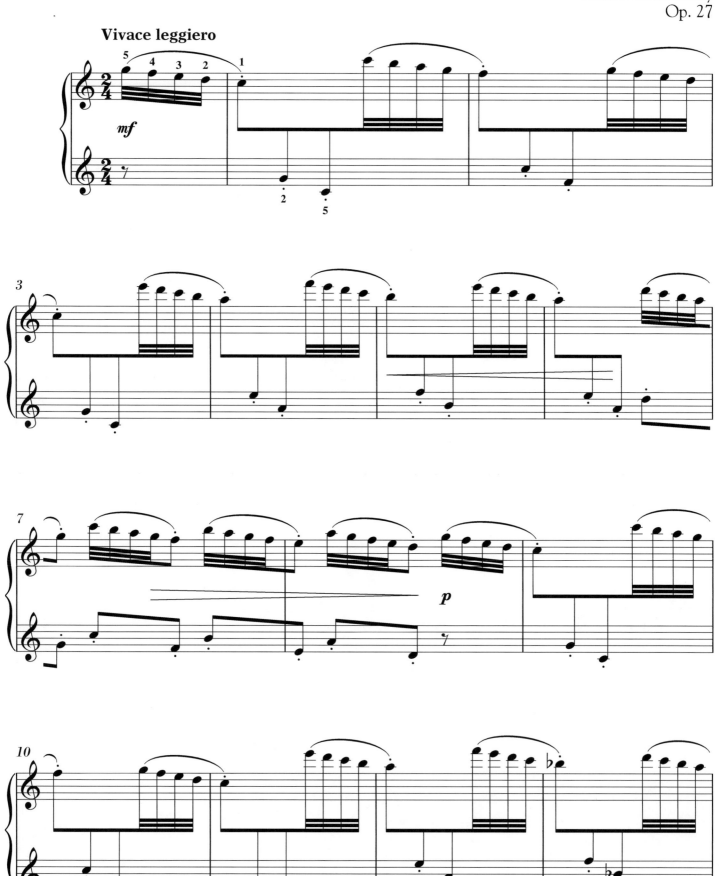

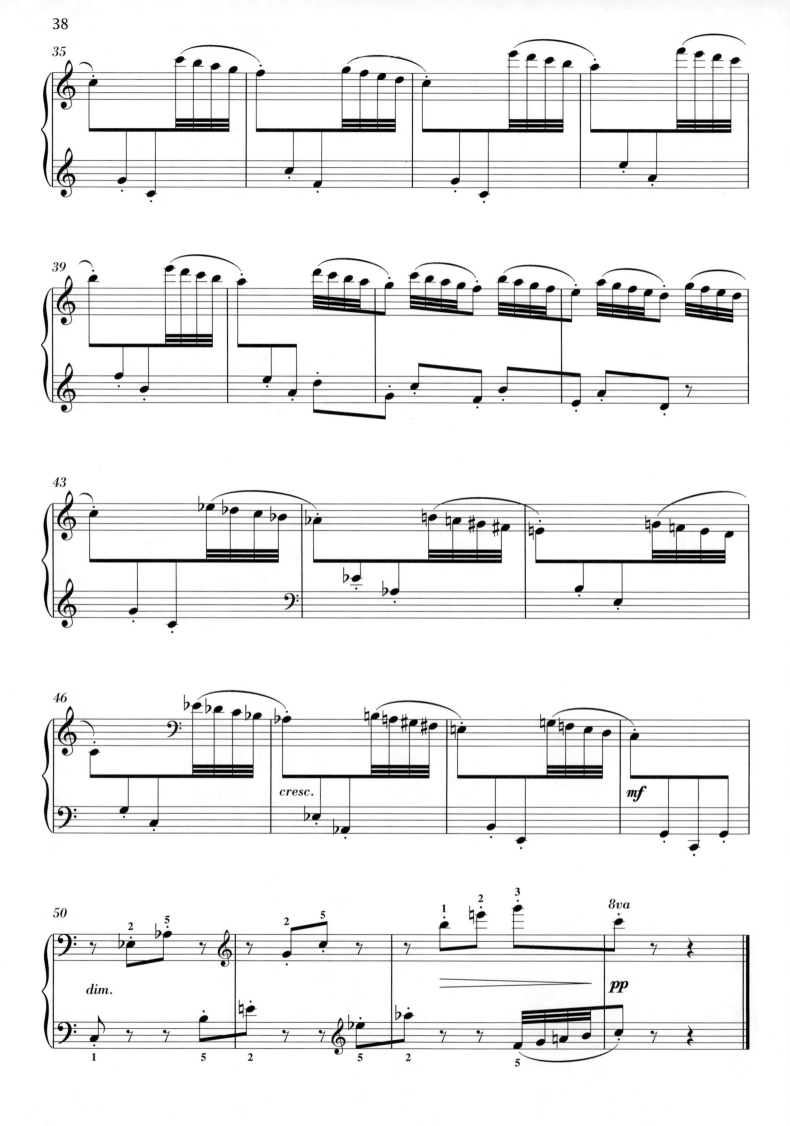

LABORUM
DULCE
LENIMEN

G. SCHIRMER

14. Scherzo

Dmitri Kabalevsky
Op. 27

15. March

Dmitri Kabalevsky
Op. 27

16. Lyric Piece

Dmitri Kabalevsky
Op. 27

Andantino con moto

17. Meadow Dance

Dmitri Kabalevsky
Op. 27

18. Sonatina

Dmitri Kabalevsky
Op. 27

19. War Dance

Dmitri Kabalevsky
Op. 27

Allegro energico

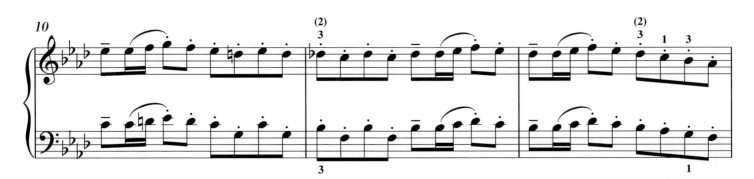

20. Fairy Tale

Dmitri Kabalevsky
Op. 27

Andantino cantabile

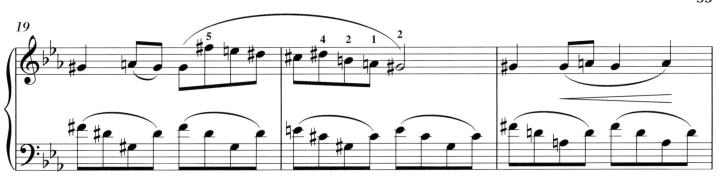

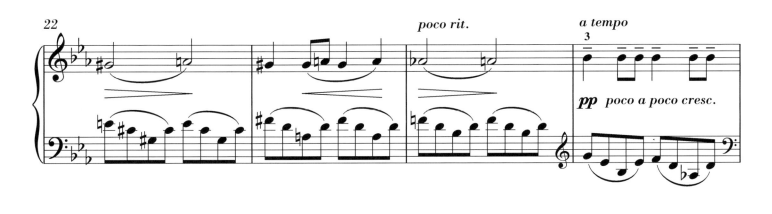

21. The Chase

Dmitri Kabalevsky
Op. 27

Allegro moderato

22. A Tale

Dmitri Kabalevsky
Op. 27

*Some editions print G-natural.

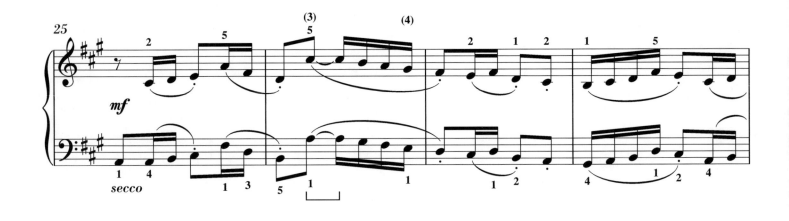

23. Snow Storm

Dmitri Kabalevsky
Op. 27

24. Etude in F Major

Dmitri Kabalevsky
Op. 27

Allegro marcato

25. Novelette

Dmitri Kabalevsky
Op. 27

26. Etude in A Major

Dmitri Kabalevsky
Op. 27

27. Dance

Dmitri Kabalevsky
Op. 27

28. Caprice

Dmitri Kabalevsky
Op. 27

Andantino

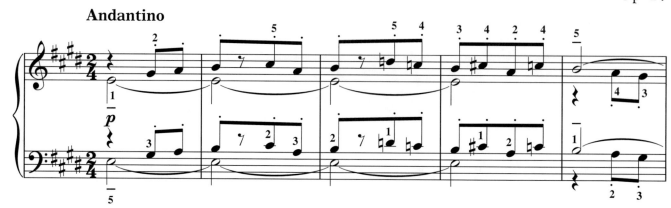

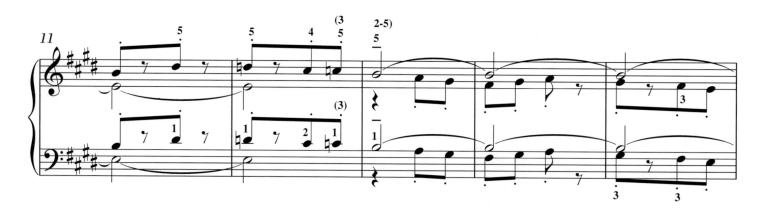

poco a poco cresc.

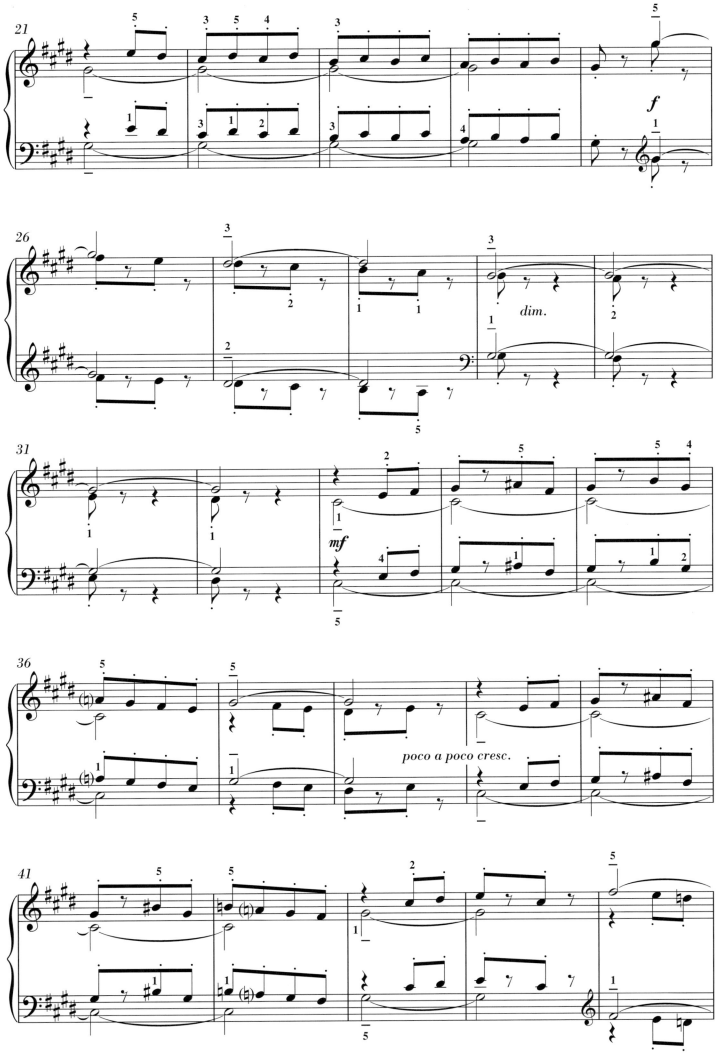

29. Song of the Cavalry

Dmitri Kabalevsky
Op. 27

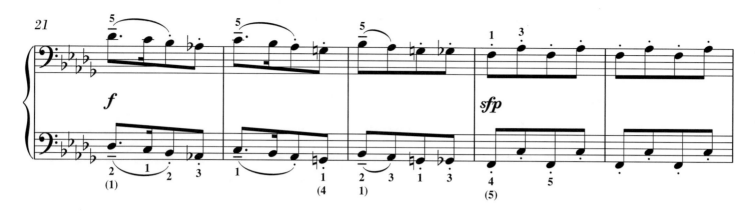

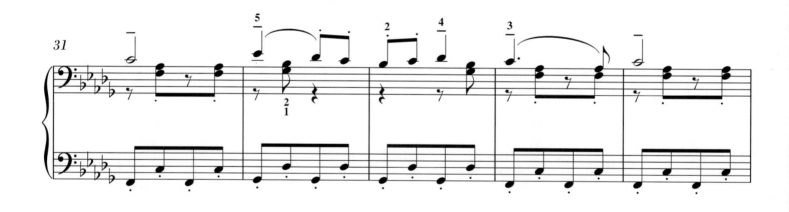

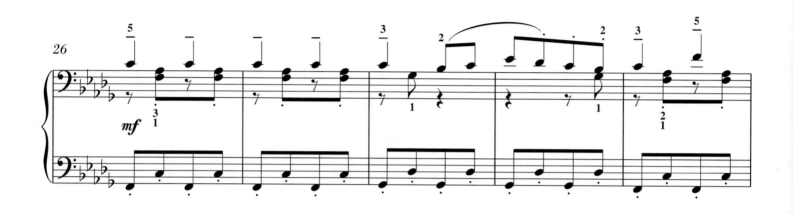

30. A Dramatic Event

Dmitri Kabalevsky
Op. 27

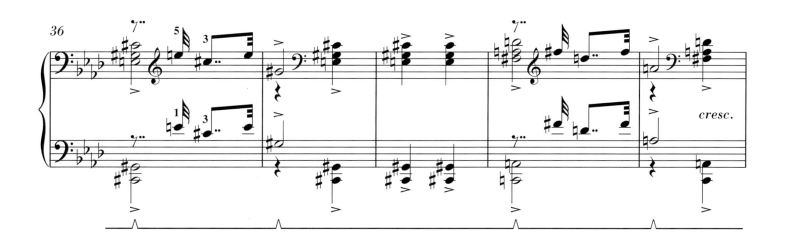

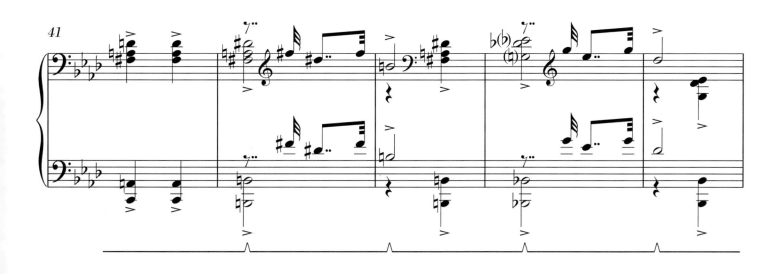

ABOUT THE RECORDING ARTIST

JEFFREY BIEGEL

Jeffrey Biegel is one of today's most respected artists having created a multi-faceted career as a pianist, recording artist, composer and arranger. His electrifying technique and mesmerizing touch have received critical acclaim and garner praise worldwide. Known for his standard-setting performances of the standard repertoire, Mr. Biegel's performances to begin the 2011–12 season include his adaptation of pop legend Neil Sedaka's *Manhattan Intermezzo* for piano and orchestra with Orchestra Kentucky, and the World Premiere of Ellen Taaffe Zwilich's *Shadows* for piano and orchestra, with the Louisiana Philharmonic Orchestra leading the consortium project with several orchestras. His recent recordings include *A Steinway Christmas Album* and *Bach On A Steinway* for the Steinway label, Leroy Anderson's Concerto in C, conducted by Leonard Slatkin with the BBC Concert Orchestra, Ellen Taaffe Zwilich's *Millennium Fantasy* and *Peanuts Gallery,* a solo CD of Vivaldi's *Four Seasons* for Naxos, *Classical Carols* for Koch and the Complete Sonatas by Mozart on the E1 label. In 2010, he performed two world premieres with the Pacific Symphony Orchestra, conducted by Carl St. Clair: Richard Danielpour's *Mirrors* for Piano and Orchestra, and, William Bolcom's *Prometheus* for Piano, Orchestra and Chorus. Mr. Biegel's *Hanukah Fantasy* for choir and piano, is published by Hal Leonard Corporation, along with Lucas Richman's orchestral arrangement with choir, published by the LeDor Group. Mr. Biegel has also created Trio21, being joined with violinist Kinga Augustyn and cellist Robert deMaine. For their inaugural season 2011–12, they will perform a new work commissioned exclusively for Trio21 by the celebrated composer, Kenneth Fuchs and record the new composition for an all-Kenneth Fuchs project for the Naxos label.

Jeffrey Biegel's career has been marked by bold, creative achievements. In the late 1990s, he initiated the first live internet recitals in New York and Amsterdam, and assembled a consortium of more than 25 orchestras to celebrate the millennium with the premiere of Ellen Taaffe Zwilich's *Millennium Fantasy* for Piano and Orchestra. In 2006, Mr. Biegel joined 18 co-commissioning orchestras for Lowell Liebermann's Concerto No. 3 for Piano and Orchestra, which was composed exclusively for him. He has played premieres of new works and arrangements with the Boston Pops, New York Pops, the American Symphony Orchestra, the Eastern Music Festival Orchestra, as well as the symphony orchestras of Minnesota, Indianapolis, and Harrisburg, among others.

Born a second-generation American, Mr. Biegel's roots are of Russian and Austrian heritage. Until the age of three, Mr. Biegel could neither hear nor speak, until corrected by surgery. The "reverse Beethoven" phenomenon can explain Mr. Biegel's life in music, having heard only vibrations in his formative years.

Mr. Biegel's published works include "The World in Our Hands" (Hal Leonard), "Christmas in a Minute" (Hal Leonard), "The Twelve Days of Christmas" (Hal Leonard), "Hey Ho, the Wind and the Rain" (Hal Leonard), "Hanukah Fantasy" (Hal Leonard), "Different Kind of Hero" (Carl Fischer), and "Elegy of Anne Boleyn" (Carl Fischer). His most recent composition is "There Shines a Light Ahead" for chorus, soprano soloist and piano. It received its World Premiere in 2011 by the Mt. Sinai High School Choir in New York.